Australian Biographical Monographs

15

Australian Biographical Monographs

Series Editor: Scott Prasser

Previous Volumes

Leonie Kramer	Damien Freeman
Margaret Guilfoyle	Anne Henderson
William McKell	David Clune
Neville Bonner	Sean Jacobs
George Reid	Luke Wallker
Robert Askin	Paul Loughnan
John Grey Gorton	Paul Williams
Stanley Melbourne Bruce	David Lee
Robert Menzies	Scott Prasser
Neville Wran	David Clune
Lindsay Thompson	William Westerman
Johannes Bjelke-Petersen	Bruce Kingston
Harold Holt	Tom Frame
Joseph Lyons	Kevin Andrews

Australian Biographical Monographs

15

Jack Lang

David Clune

Connor Court Publishing

Australian Biographical Monographs 15
Jack Lang by David Clune
Published in 2022 by Connor Court Publishing Pty Ltd

Copyright © David Clune 2022

All rights reserved. No part of this book may be reproduced or transmitted in any form or by any means, electronic or mechanical, including photo copying, recording or by any information storage and retrieval system, without prior permission in writing from the publisher.

Connor Court Publishing Pty Ltd
PO Box 7257
Redland Bay QLD 4165
sales@connorcourt.com
www.connorcourt.com
Phone 0497-900-685

Printed in Australia

ISBN: 9781922815019

Cover image:
Jack Lang, Australian politician, demonstrating his public-speaking technique, circa 1930, National Library of Australia, Fairfax, Wikipedia Commons.

*In the race of life, always back self-interest;
at least you know it's trying.*

Jack Lang, *Sydney Morning Herald*, 10 June 2013

Series overview

The Connor Court *Australian Biographical Monograph Series* focusses on important Australian political leaders and other major figures. It seeks to provide an overview for those who are unfamiliar with the subject, and to highlight the person's particular importance, controversies around them and their contribution to Australia's progress.

The monographs are scholarly rather than academic in focus, placing emphasis on a clear narrative, but with careful attention to sources to ensure views expressed are appropriately supported.

The Series was initiated because of the decline in the study of Australian history at our schools and universities and the consequential lack of knowledge or, even worse, distorting of views, of some of Australia's leading historical figures who deserve to be remembered, understood for their achievements, and, as each volume also highlights, their flaws.

Jack Lang, Labor Premier of New South Wales from 1925-7 and 1930-32, was until his death in 1975, a martyr for some in his party and reviled by others. This biography highlights the disruption he was responsible for, less to his opponents and more to his own side. Indeed, his relatively few legislative and policy successes are outweighed by the damage he caused. Today, Lang is better remembered for his notoriety rather than his achievements. It was left to others like Bill McKell, who became Premier in 1941, to rebuild the Labor Party, and, more importantly, bring it back to its true mission of helping those in need rather than indulging in self-serving political crusades of the type pursued by Lang.

This new monograph by Dr David Clune OAM assesses Lang's career and brings into clear focus his flawed record. Dr Clune, long-time Manager of the New South Wales Parliament's Research Service and the Parliament's Historian, and author of studies in this series on New South Wales Labor Premiers Neville Wran and Bill McKell, puts Jack Lang into proper perspective.

-- Scott Prasser

(Editor, *Australian Biographical Monographs*)

Preface

Although I never met Jack Lang, I did watch his funeral cortege pass by from the verandah of Parliament House on its way to St Mary's Cathedral. I remember remarking to a long-serving member of the parliamentary attendant staff that we would be going home early as the house had adjourned as a mark of respect. His response: he was good for the worker to the last!

I have been influenced in my interpretation of Lang by conversations with Sir William McKell and Reg Downing. Bede Nairn's monumental study of Lang, *The 'Big Fella'*, is still the definitive work. Other major sources I have drawn on are Heather Radi and Peter Spearritt's pioneering 1977 volume *Jack Lang*, Boris Schedvin's *Australian and the Great Depression*, and Andrew Moore's *The Secret Army and the Premier* (see the Select Bibliography for more details on sources).

I would like to thank Judy Butlin, Milton Cockburn, Brian Dale, Carl Green and Greig Tillotson for reading the manuscript. I am particularly indebted to Walter Hamilton who spent much time and effort preparing a challenging critique which deepened my understanding of Lang and the Depression. The responsibility for errors and omissions remains my own.

At Connor Court, I would once again like to acknowledge the assistance of Scott Prasser and Anthony Cappello.

David Clune

July 2021

Jack Lang

Jack Lang is one of the best known of New South Wales Premiers, leaving a legend of mythical proportions: the strongman who stood up for the workers against the bankers until he was stabbed in the back by the King's representative. He was also one of the most damaging in terms of his impact on the economy, politics and social cohesion of New South Wales.

Lang's leadership style – autocratic, messianic, radical, destructive – had a profound influence on New South Wales Labor, although in a negative way. After a decade of vicious faction-fighting and lack of electoral success under Lang, the New South Wales Branch, guided by his successor as Labor Leader and Premier, Bill McKell, in 1941 captured and subsequently colonised the centre ground of politics.[1] Labor became increasingly known for its moderate, pragmatic, electorally appealing style. Memories of the chaotic Lang era and the resultant long, cold years in the wilderness strengthened the resolve of many in the Party to ensure there was no major split in the 1950s, as happened federally and in Victoria and Queensland. The backlash against Lang was one reason why Labor governed in New South Wales from 1941-65.

Early life and career[2]

John Thomas Lang was born on 21 December 1876 in inner Sydney, the sixth of the ten children of James, a watchmaker from Edinburgh, and his Irish wife, Mary. Due to his father's financial and health problems, young Jack spent four years with relatives in Bairnsdale, Victoria, a not uncommon arrangement at the time. He attended the local Catholic school. Returning to Sydney in his early teens, Jack attended night school for about a year and worked at various manual jobs.

On 14 March 1896, Lang married Hilda Bredt, the stepdaughter of WH McNamara who had a bookshop in Castlereagh Street. It was a well-known gathering place and centre of activity for Sydney leftists. Although Jack and Hilda lived after their marriage with the McNamara's, little of their socialism seems to have rubbed off on their son-in-law. The Langs had seven children, one of whom, John Christian, briefly succeeded his father as a New South Wales MLA.

Lang had an unusual early career for someone who became a Labor messiah, described in the 1930s as "greater than Lenin".[3] Initially working at unskilled jobs, Jack aspired to white collar ones. In 1893 he was a junior in an accountant's office and three years later a real estate agent's clerk at Auburn, a semi-rural area in Sydney's west which was rapidly becoming urbanised and industrialised. In 1901, Lang established an estate agency and auctioneering business in partnership with HH Dawes.

Lang prospered as Auburn grew. He bought a grand local house and dressed like a gentleman. His prosperity, outward respectability and active interest in capitalism would have made him a good fit for the conservative side of politics. However, his humble background and Catholicism would have militated against this. The anti-Labor parties were rigidly sectarian.

Lang joined the Labor Party at the turn of the century and rose steadily to local prominence. Peter Spearritt has commented on the anomaly of an aspiring Labor politician finding "acceptance within his community and his Political Labor League while conducting a business associated with exploitation of the many members of the working class who could not afford to buy their own homes".[4]

In 1907, Lang was elected an Alderman on Auburn Council and was Mayor from 1909-11. In December 1913, he was the Labor candidate for the local State electorate of Granville. Lang won the seat from the sitting Liberal MLA with 52 per cent of the primary vote. He was to represent the area in State Parliament until 1946.

Lang never had a consistent ideology, other than promoting himself by any means possible - although he had residual sympathy for the working class as a result of his upbringing. Lang was gifted with native cunning, an instinctive sense for the main chance, personal charisma, and an impressive physical appearance. He refined this into a magnetic, demagogic appeal. Bede Nairn has said that Lang had a "crude but effective public speaking style: rasping voice, snarling mouth, flailing hands, sentences and phrases punctuated by long pauses".[5] Tall, solidly built, handsome, with a jutting jaw that personified pugnacity and purpose, he was known as "the Big Fella".

Lang had determination, energy and ability but lacked intellectual rigour and depth. Rabble-rousing cliches were more his style than studied conclusions. He was not overly encumbered by scruples or principles. Personal loyalties and obligations counted for little in his egocentric world. Lang had a permanent sense of grievance as a result of his deprived childhood: "get square" with life, no matter how, was an over-riding trait. Bullying, mendacity, and megalomania were increasingly dominant characteristics. Lang had a cold, forbidding personality. He had admirers and disciples, but few, if any, friends.

Parliamentarian

In October 1910, James McGowen became the first Labor Premier of New South Wales. In June 1913, he was succeeded by his Attorney-General, William Arthur Holman, a man of quicksilver brilliance. Under Holman, Labor was convincingly re-elected in December 1913, although the government's ability to enact legislation was still impeded by its lack of a majority in the Legislative Council.

Lang entered State Parliament at a time of increasing tensions within the Labor Party. Many in the extra-parliamentary party were impatient with what they considered to be the slow pace of implementation of Labor policy. In 1916, the dissident Industrial Section took control of the State Executive. Holman, rather than trying to placate and explain the difficulties of reform in office, became increasingly confrontational and intolerant of criticism.

The First World War threw petrol on the flames of this volatile mix. Holman and Prime Minister Billy Hughes supported conscription. The Labor Party repudiated them both. Holman and most of his ministers left Labor and in November 1916 formed a government with their former Liberal Party opponents as the Nationalist Party.

Ernest Durack became Leader of the Opposition but was soon succeeded by the capable and respected John Storey. Lang was anti-Holman and anti-conscription but was not prominent in the struggle. At the March 1917 election, Holman was re-elected as Premier at the head of a Nationalist Government.

Within the Labor Party, the conscription split increased the existing bitter factionalism. As so many MPs had departed, it re-enforced the determination of the extra-parliamentary party to exert more control over the politicians. It also increased the strength of the left. Nonetheless, in 1919 the powerful Australian Workers' Union (AWU), under its ambitious, aggressive and ruthless leader, Jack Bailey (an MLA from 1918-25), vanquished the radicals and took control of the Executive.

Bede Nairn has said that, in Parliament, Lang was at first "strangely subdued",

> almost as if he wanted to recuperate after 13 years of battling his way to success in the risky and demanding business of land and house dealing in an insular society and to the top of a parochial section of a turbulent political party ... He was a little over-awed ... But at heart he respected and even liked the structure and procedure involved in a parliamentary system derived from Westminster. This acceptance was a main source of his determination to prove himself in his new milieu ... [6]

On 3 March 1914, Lang moved the Address-in-Reply to the Governor's Speech at the opening of Parliament. It was an honour usually bestowed on a promising new backbencher. His remarks were straightforward, factual and unadorned. Making the most of his business expertise, he devoted much of his speech to financial matters: the deficit, income tax, stamp duties, and banking. Lang also advocated more public housing, particularly in his electorate.[7] Ironically, as Premier, he achieved nothing in this area.[8] Government finance and local disadvantage were continuing themes in Lang's speeches.

Lang was a hard-working, diligent MLA who took Parliament seriously and mastered its forms and procedures. As he gained experience and confidence he became a frequent contributor in the House across a wide range of subjects, often focussing on issues of concern to Labor such as industrial relations. In the 1919 session, his contributions as listed in the Hansard index fill just over three columns, only slightly less than that of Premier Holman. Lang's oratorical weapon was the bludgeon rather than the rapier: he piled up facts, criticisms and accusations. There was little hint of ideas or vision. He was a frequent interjector and was rarely lost for a response to one.

Lang's remarks often featured insinuations and personal attacks, as in this contribution to the debate on the Supply Bill in August 1917:

> Parliament is not told what was spent last year; we are merely told that so much was estimated to be spent during that year. The result is that this country is being governed by a few highly paid men in the [public] service who sit behind the bar of the House whenever the estimates are presented, and will not tell the country how the money is spent. It could easily be done. I have listened to some honourable members, who prate about their loyalty and how their hearts bleed for their country. They would be better employed in letting the country know what has become of its money ... Last year when the estimates were before us and the Premier [Holman] was here I asked him if it was not a fair thing that we should know where the money went. He thought it an estimable idea and said so in his most courteous and convincing manner. There is no doubt about his being a perfect gentleman. There is no doubt about his air of sincerity. He carried me away on that occasion to believe that what I suggested was a fair thing; he said he would try to see if there could not be three columns, one showing the amount voted in the previous year; a second showing the amount spent; and a third showing the estimate for the year. What is the use of a man saying he will do that when we find at the end of twelve months he is only a faker and a fooler.[9]

Lang's darker side was occasionally evident. In

September 1919, he physically assaulted Housing Minister DR Hall, a Labor conscriptionist, during a division.[10]

The conscription split worked in Lang's favour as roughly half of the Labor parliamentary party departed, including most of the talented. In 1916 he became Caucus Secretary and the following year Opposition Whip. Lang was developing a canny understanding of the Labor Party and the Caucus and how to manipulate both to his advantage.

Leader of the Opposition

The Nationalist Government changed the electoral system from single member constituencies to proportional representation for the 1920 election. The stated aim was to decrease the influence of party machines by giving voters a greater choice of candidate. It signally failed to do this but did create political instability by electing governments with miniscule majorities in 1920, 1922 and 1925.

In a demonstration of Labor's electoral resilience in New South Wales, in spite of the upheaval of the conscription split it was able to take office after the March 1920 election. The numbers in the Legislative Assembly were, in effect, 45 all (taking account of Independents). However, as the Progressive Party (the precursor of the Country Party) was not prepared to enter into a definite agreement to support the Nationalists, John Storey, as the leader of the largest party in the house, was commissioned as premier. The incumbent Nationalist Speaker, Daniel Levy, agreed to remain in the Chair, giving the Government a majority of one.

The 1920-22 Labor Government was doomed from the beginning. As well as being constrained by its narrow hold on power and the conservative-dominated Legislative Council, Storey was suffering from chronic kidney disease which claimed him on 5 October 1921. He was succeeded by his Deputy, James Dooley, who was overwhelmed by the difficulties he faced. There was division in cabinet and Jack Bailey was a source of intrigue and destabilisation.[11] It is not surprising that the Dooley Government achieved little, further increasing dissatisfaction in the extra-parliamentary party.

Lang was a supporter of Storey. His solid performance, status in Caucus, and specialisation in financial matters led to his appointment as Treasurer. With typical vindictiveness, Lang drove out his permanent head, JW Holliman. Lang had previously attacked Holliman in the Legislative Assembly, accusing him of being over-powerful and over-paid.[12] Nairn has observed that Lang "could not abide any rival, least of all a subordinate".[13]

As Treasurer, Lang performed with "solid

competence by the standards of the day, winning a reputation for determination and level-headedness amongst his colleagues which offset the displeasure of unions affected by his financial stringency". The Opposition "praised the clarity and informativeness of his budget statements".[14]

The Dooley Government was unsurprisingly defeated at an early election in March 1922 and the Nationalists under Sir George Fuller took office. Dooley was re-elected Labor leader; Lang contested the deputy's position but was easily defeated by WF Dunn, MLA for Mudgee. The election loss plunged Labor into further factional strife.

The Bailey/AWU Executive was notorious for corruption, thuggery and ballot-rigging. Dooley described it as a "gang of uncouth crooks".[15] He was the loser in the power struggle and was expelled from the Party in March 1923. The New South Wales Executive installed an AWU ally, Greg McGirr, as his replacement. The anti-Bailey group appealed to the Federal Labor Executive, which intervened and appointed Dunn interim leader pending resolution of the situation by the 1923 annual conference.

A coalition of parliamentarians, union moderates, and the left-wing Miners' Federation, led by Albert Willis, overthrew the Bailey Executive at the June 1923 conference. A Christian socialist, Willis became Party President. Bailey retreated into surly opposition. He formed an unlikely alliance with a group of far left unionists, the "Trades Hall Reds", led by Labor Council Secretary Jock Garden, an unstable extremist and opportunist who had been a foundation member of the Australian Communist Party in 1920.[16]

A key organiser for Dooley, Lang's influential role at the conference had won him support. Willis was now an important ally, as were moderate industrialists from the Trades Hall. Lang had no natural affinity with the union movement but recognised it was the key to success in the Labor Party.

Dooley was reinstated as leader but indicated that he would not continue in the position. Peter Loughlin, a popular and influential rural MLA, was a strong contender but decided not to stand, backing Lang instead. Dunn was a candidate but had lost support by agreeing to become acting leader. On 31 July 1923, Lang defeated Dunn for the leadership, 21 votes to 11; Loughlin defeated Dunn for the deputy leadership, 19 to 13. Lang had "seized the leadership of the Parliamentary Labor Party through a fortuitous set of circumstances. The power he acquired remained correspondingly tenuous".[17]

Lang's first task was to persuade the electorate that Labor had rid itself of the corruption of the

Bailey era and Communist influence. A committee set up by the 1923 New South Wales conference found Bailey guilty of the manipulation of party ballots and he was expelled as a result. In 1923, the Executive banned Communists from Labor Party membership. Garden was expelled when he refused to sign a declaration that he was not a member of any other party. The 1924 annual conference confirmed both expulsions.[18]

Lang quickly alienated many of his colleagues. On 27 June 1924, he was challenged for the Leadership by Tom Mutch, MLA for Botany. According to Nairn, Mutch had been appalled by Lang's behaviour "which included constant insults and taunts to MLAs who had crossed him, even trivially. Lang's bullying and individualism had in fact split the Caucus virtually in half, and many ambitious members and others who refused to toady to him were anxious to take the chance to get rid of him".[19] Lang just survived, 18 votes to 17.

The Fuller Government's record was reactionary. Most of the first Labor Government's state enterprises were closed down or sold off. Recurrent expenditure was low and the public works program was restricted. The 48-hour week was re-introduced, rural workers and public servants were removed from the jurisdiction of the Arbitration Court, and public sector employees had their wages reduced.[20]

The Progressives had again refused to go into Coalition with the Nationalists and there was friction between the two parties. The Fuller Government's reputation was damaged by internal divisions. Sectarian tensions were high at this time. The Protestant Federation was powerful in the Nationalist Party and many influential government MLAs publicly expressed allegiance to it. Fuller, a Presbyterian, was not an active supporter of the Protestant Federation and had no desire to promote sectarian strife. However, the extreme Protestant faction in the government was too powerful for him to control. The main force behind it was Minister of Justice TJ Ley. A psychopathic criminal, he was responsible for one actual and several probable murders. Ley emerged as a source of dissension in the government and there were rumours that he was intriguing to replace Fuller as Premier.

The Nationalists' prospects for the 30 May 1925 election were not good. The economy was in recession and unemployment and social distress were widespread. The influence of sectarianism had begun to wane. Ley's blatant attempt to stir up the issue may, in fact, have been counter-productive and alienated significant portions of the electorate. The Fuller Government's actions had lost it the support of trade unionists and public servants. All Fuller had to offer was sound finance and anti-Communism.

Lang, by contrast, offered an attractive program: widows' pensions; assistance for the unemployed; the abolition of high school fees; restoration of the 44-hour week; increased expenditure on public works. An effective campaigner, he astutely exploited the government's weaknesses. Labor won 46 of the 90 seats and had the support of a Protestant Labor MLA and an Independent.

First Premiership (1925-27)

Lang became Premier and Treasurer on 17 June 1925. In a repeat of the 1920 clash with Holliman, he forced out the permanent head of Treasury, Bertram Stevens. Stevens had the last laugh when he succeeded Lang as Premier in 1932. Willis resigned as Secretary of the Miners' Federation to become Leader of the Government in the Legislative Council. He was close to Lang and his control of the influential *Labor Daily* made him even more powerful. Lang was later to take over the *Labor Daily* from the Miners' Federation and make it his mouthpiece.

After the unsatisfactory performance of the last two Labor governments, there was a widespread feeling that the Party had to deliver this time. The newly elected MLA for Balmain, HV "Bert" Evatt – later a bitter opponent of Lang – said in his maiden speech in August 1925:

> The trouble in the past has been, and the public has realised it, that a government has been elected, but has not commenced steadily and consistently to carry out the Labor platform. I am satisfied that this will never be said of the present administration... [W]e are determined to make our ideals practical and effective; to see that they are not merely academic, but are transformed into legislation.[21]

Lang exploited this attitude to consolidate his power. Here, at last, was a determined, forceful Labor Premier dedicated to implementing the platform, unlike previous politicians who had betrayed the Labor Party. The unions and branches responded with adulation. Lang realised that he could use his increasingly fanatical following to dominate the parliamentary party.

Lang pushed through legislation that conservatives saw as extremely radical. Speaking on a bill to extend the local government franchise to all ratepayers, JCL Fitzpatrick (MLA for Bathurst) accused the government of proposing to "hand over to the tender mercies of every Tom, Dick, and Harry, and to every derelict in the community who never had and never will have a copper, the control of the destinies of the municipalities of New South Wales".[22] The Member for Oxley, TH Hill, described the Widows' Pensions Bill as the "most soul destroying, poisonous bill which has ever been submitted to this House. It is nothing more nor less than communistic legislation ... a poison with which you are going to inoculate the general public, and by which you will ultimately bring about the absolute destruction of the self-reliant spirit".[23]

Lang's behaviour in the Legislative Assembly was a source of much criticism. In March 1926, for example, the *Sydney Morning Herald* complained of "the studied insolence, the calculated and brutal indifference to the elementary courtesies of parliament which have been characteristic of this session".[24] Lang was something of a chameleon in parliament. He could argue his case logically and persuasively with just the right emotional overtones when he chose to do so. On other occasions he adopted an aggressive, bullying manner and belittled his opponents with cheap jibes and snide remarks. Nairn describes Lang's parliamentary performances as marked by "obsessive abuse and misrepresentations".[25]

Labor's lack of a majority in the Legislative Council was a serious problem. The Government won 55 per cent of divisions from 1925-27; the succeeding conservative government (1927-30) won 95 per cent.[26] However, compromises were sometimes negotiated that allowed truncated versions of legislation to be enacted. Useful measures were passed in the areas of: fair rents, workers' compensation, working hours, industrial arbitration, widows' pensions, child endowment, and marketing arrangements of benefit to small farmers. Given the constraints the Lang government was under, it was a solid record, particularly compared to the Storey/Dooley period.[27] Although much of the hard work had been done by his ministers, Lang took the credit and used it to bolster his heroic image.

On 21 December 1925, Governor Sir Dudley de Chair reluctantly agreed to Lang's request for the appointment of 25 Labor Legislative Councillors. A condition was that these appointments were not to be used to abolish the Council. In accordance with British precedent, de Chair considered that Lang needed an electoral mandate before taking such a major step. Abolition was long-standing Labor policy and in January 1926 Lang reneged on his undertaking to De Chair and introduced an abolition bill. It was defeated in February by 47 votes to 41. Two Labor MLCs crossed the floor and five abstained. All were expelled from the Labor Party.[28] Lang then demanded more appointments from the Governor. De Chair, feeling "deceived and disgusted" by Lang's behaviour, refused them.[29] Lang's strident denunciations of the Council and his abolition attempt increased the strength of his following among the Labor rank and file.

Lang's first government ended in disarray, mainly due to disputes with his colleagues. Nairn notes that in office Lang's deficiencies were even more obvious: "Now, his disloyalty to his colleagues, and his unjustifiable willingness to claim for himself...

virtually all the credit for the admirable record of the government, gave added offence to many ministers and MLAs".[30]

Many parliamentarians, particularly from country areas, were disturbed by the increasing leftward turn of the Party, the influence of Willis, and Lang's autocratic control. This culminated in a leadership challenge on 14 September 1926 by Lands Minister and Deputy Leader Peter Loughlin, MLA for Goulburn, a Catholic and strong anti-Communist. Loughlin had initially been a supporter of Lang but, as with many others, close acquaintance led to disenchantment. The result was a tied vote. After intensive study of the Caucus rules, it was decided the next day that as Lang had not actually been deposed he remained leader.[31]

In November 1926, a special Labor conference came to Lang's aid by ruling that the leader would in future be appointed by the party conference, not Caucus. Loughlin resigned from cabinet and subsequently the Labor Party in protest. Two other country Labor MLAs, Vernon Goodin and Robert Gillies, who shared Loughlin's concerns about Lang and the influence of urban leftists, joined him in a rebel rural group. The trio threatened to vote for a no confidence motion against Lang on 22 November. Their votes would have brought the Lang Government down but they abstained at the last moment.

An agreement was negotiated with Goodin and Gillies who, unlike Loughlin, had not left the Labor Party. In return for a number of concessions, they agreed to support the government. This gave Lang a renewed, if fragile, hold on office. However, the April 1927 annual conference, repudiated the Goodin/Gillies pact, mainly due to the intervention of Willis, whose removal was part of the agreement. This precipitated another crisis when Lang, in a typically two-faced move, backed the conference decision. Cabinet and the majority of Caucus rejected it.[32]

Lang was by now at odds with all of his ministers except Willis. He decided that an early election was the best way out of his difficulties. Most of the cabinet, however, opposed the request. Governor de Chair believed that the government was in such a chaotic state that a dissolution was necessary. He allowed Lang to resign, be re-commissioned and reconstruct his cabinet on condition that he hold an election as soon as possible and act in caretaker mode in the interim. A new cabinet consisting entirely of Lang supporters was sworn in on 27 May. Only three of the former ministers remained, one of whom (Bill McKell) was subsequently dropped for disloyalty. Lang again requested a dissolution, this time with the support of cabinet, which De Chair granted. Parliament was dissolved on 7 September 1927.[33]

Lang's enemies dubbed his new ministry of sycophants the "Scabinet". It was too much for many in Caucus and a split ensued. On 30 May, 24 MLAs repudiated Lang and elected Tom Mutch as Leader.[34] To complicate matters, the Executive had split into rival factions, one backed by Federal Labor and the AWU and presided over by F Conroy; the other, under WH "Bull" Seale, supporting Lang and Willis. The majority of unions and branches backed Lang.

The Federal Labor Executive convened a special conference held in July 1927 to resolve the situation. Lang had the advantage as the Federal Party did not want division in New South Wales to jeopardise its chances in the 1928 Federal election. It was a complete triumph for Lang. According to Nairn, he was now "parliamentary leader independent of Caucus; he could ... chose his own cabinet, if he wanted to; and could ... select candidates for the Legislative Council. And through his vast personal following could virtually control the preselection of candidates for the Legislative Assembly. His heroic stature seemed invulnerable".[35]

The election held on 8 October 1927 saw a return to single member constituencies, with an optional preferential voting system. Labor was defeated and Thomas Bavin took office at the head of a Nationalist/Country Party Coalition Ministry. In a 90 seat House, the government had 46 seats and there were two Independent Nationalists. It was surprisingly narrow defeat given the divisions and crises that had marked Lang's first term.

The 1927 election has been described as atypical:

> It is generally assumed that political parties in liberal democratic states are social machines for winning elections and thus gaining power. This does not seem to have been the main purpose in Lang's mind when he resigned in May 1927 and precipitated an election. Lang resigned knowing full well he was likely to lose the ensuing election. His resignation was designed not to maximise electoral support for the ALP, but to consolidate the control of Willis and himself over the party machine. In fact, he was successful in this – and the electoral victory was postponed only for three years.[36]

Opposition again

Lang took revenge on his enemies by depriving most of them of their preselections. This ensured he had a more compliant Caucus after the 1927 election. Labor MLAs realised that if they were to have a future they needed to be obsequiously loyal to Lang. The branches and most unions were now strong adherents. Jock Garden abandoned the Communist Party, re-joined Labor in 1929 and became a fervent Langite. Lang ruled through a shadowy "Inner Group" of henchmen that controlled party decisions and preselections. Key members were JJ Graves, PJ Keller, JB "Plugger" Martin, and Garden.

The already boiling cauldron of Labor factionalism was further heated by the advent of EG "Ted" Theodore in New South Wales politics. Labor Premier of Queensland from 1919-25, the highly regarded Theodore entered Federal Parliament by winning the seat of Dalley in inner Sydney in 1927. When Labor under James Scullin won the 1929 Federal election, Theodore became Deputy Prime Minister and Treasurer. He had skilfully masterminded the campaign in New South Wales. Theodore was strongly aligned with the AWU and was seen by Lang as a dangerous rival. Rightly so, as Theodore had grand plans to displace Lang as the powerbroker in New South Wales and then replace Scullin as Prime Minister. The relationship between Lang and Theodore was like that of two scorpions in a bottle. The April 1930 annual conference was a test of strength – it unequivocally showed that Theodore's aims were unrealistic and confirmed the Lang dictatorship.[37]

As well as Theodore and the AWU, Lang faced opposition from the far left in the form of the Socialisation Units. They had been formed in 1930 to bring about "socialism in our time" and were an increasingly powerful faction. The Inner Group saw them as a threat to its control. Lang was concerned that their radicalism and links with the

Communist Party would jeopardise his election prospects. The Units were liquidated by the Inner Group at the 1933 annual conference.[38]

It was Tom Bavin's misfortune to become Premier as the Great Depression started to bite. Bavin's ideology was that of a 19th century liberal. He had been private secretary to Edmund Barton and Alfred Deakin, both life-long friends. As Fuller's Attorney-General and chief lieutenant he had passed pioneering anti-monopoly laws. However, when confronted by the crisis of the Depression Bavin fell back on orthodox financial policy: balancing the budget, cutting public expenditure and reducing wages. The Bavin Government's reputation was damaged by a long-running, bitter dispute in the northern coalfields. In a confrontation with police on 16 December 1929, a miner was shot dead by police. Bavin was accused of being overly sympathetic to the colliery owners.[39]

It was a perfect situation for Lang to exploit. He styled himself as the selfless servant of the labour movement – a sturdy warrior doing battle for the workers. Most fell into line behind their champion.

In the 1930 election campaign, Lang promised to maintain the standard of living, reduce working hours, and increase unemployment relief and social security payments. Boris Schedvin has commented on the contrast between the rival programs:

> The Nationalists' was a dull academic affair, bent on the correction of past [economic] misdeeds. Labor's promised return to the land of milk and honey; the unemployed and those threatened with dismissal and wage reductions were not interested in whether this was possible – they were willing to grasp at any straw.[40]

A Labor advertisement unsubtly said: "Gloom under the Bavin Nationalist Government. Joy if you vote for the Lang Labor Government. For brighter times change the Government".[41] Labor won a landslide victory at the 25 October 1930 election, with 55 seats to the Coalition's 35.

Second Premiership (1930-32)

The Depression in Australia peaked during Lang's second term. Schedvin has calculated that gross national product fell "by 9 per cent in 1929/30, by 18 per cent in 1930/31, and by a further 7 per cent in the trough year of 1931/32. Unemployment, which had averaged 8 per cent during the 1920s as a whole, rose to 10 per cent in 1929, and then climbed steeply to 18 per cent in 1930, to 27 per cent in 1931, and reached a peak of 28 per cent in 1932".[42] The New South Wales Government "was the first to face seriously the issue of rapidly declining national income, rising unemployment and shrinking taxable capacity ... By the early months of 1930 it was anticipated the New South Wales deficit would exceed £3 million; the actual deficit in the end amounted to £4.8 million".[43] According to figures supplied to the Commonwealth Statistician by trade unions, unemployment in New South Wales reached 32 per cent in 1932.[44]

The Australian economy was particularly vulnerable when the Depression hit:

> A high level of debt on the London money market, combined with a heavy reliance on rural commodities for foreign exchange made it hypersensitive to overseas conditions. When the shock waves from the Wall Street collapse reached Australia via London early in 1930 they brought an abrupt halt to the relatively easy credit that until then had serviced the national debt. In the first quarter of 1930 this was compounded by an alarming reverse in the terms of trade.[45]

Australian governments faced a financial crisis due to "falling revenue, rapidly diminishing reserves and loan obligations that no longer could be met from new borrowing".[46]

Few leaders could have been less suited to the demands of the times than Lang. His second term was, in fact, to end in the greatest crisis New South Wales society and politics have faced. On the positive side, Lang legislated to protect debtors facing foreclosure. He restricted evictions and the sale of tenants' furniture to recover unpaid rent. The unemployment relief tax on wages was increased. The Farmers' Relief Board was established to provide protection from creditors and rehabilitation for heavily indebted primary producers. However, Lang's antipathetic, divisive side was dominant.

In August 1930, the Commonwealth and all State premiers, on the advice of Sir Otto Niemeyer of the Bank of England who had come to Australia to advise on the economic crisis, adopted the Melbourne agreement. The main aim was balanced budgets to be achieved through cuts in public expenditure. Lang attacked Niemeyer and the Melbourne agreement, although in the 1930 election campaign he rejected debt repudiation, realising it was electorally controversial.[47]

As economic and political difficulties multiplied, the Melbourne agreement became increasingly unsustainable. In response, Prime Minster Jim Scullin convened a meeting with the State premiers in February 1931. Schedvin has said that Treasurer Theodore opened the conference with a brilliant speech advocating "the abandonment of traditional thinking and the adoption of a new and expansionary policy which would stimulate production, reduce unemployment and restore prices to the 1929 level. It was a moderate and sophisticated performance, and was conspicuous for its quality and the fundamental grasp of banking procedure; but it clearly was not understood by the Premiers".[48] As well as lack of comprehension of his advanced ideas, Theodore had to contend with "a hostile Senate, a deeply orthodox chairman of the Commonwealth Bank, Sir Robert Gibson, and an electorate resistant to novelty in economic policy".[49]

Lang was alarmed. He could not allow his rival Theodore to dominate the conference and undermine his carefully created image as the fearless fighter who stood up for the ordinary worker against the power of the financiers. He countered with the Lang Plan. The main features were suspension of interest payments to British bondholders, the reduction of interest on government loans in Australia, and replacing the gold standard with a nebulous "goods standard" based upon the wealth of Australia. Scullin, Theodore, and the other Premiers rejected the Lang Plan.

There was a legitimate economic debate between conservatives, who believed Australia was "living beyond its means and must accept a reduction in living standards", and some moderates and many radicals who believed "action should be taken to halt the decline in production and employment".[50] Rather than entering constructively into this debate, Lang contributed "gangrenous afflictions".[51]

Schedvin has commented that the Lang Plan was "cleverly devised to divert the masses. It offered 'economic rainbows' to chase – and it is not difficult to appreciate how appealing these rainbows must have appeared to the army of unemployed and those threatened with unemployment in the bleak and confused days of 1931".[52] Nairn describes it as essentially a political attempt to place Lang at the head of Labor at the expense of the Scullin Government but "Lang and his followers propagated it as an economic panacea, although it was deficient theoretically and impossible to translate into legislative and administrative form".[53]

Economist David Clark has observed: "A cunning politician Lang certainly was – an original or even prescient economic thinker he was not".[54] After a detailed re-evaluation of the Lang Plan, Clark concluded:

> The belief in Lang as a great practical economist, as a serious precursor of Keynes, as a man ahead of his time, does not stand up to scrutiny. The mysteries of economics to many lay persons enabled Lang to project such images of himself without him being seriously questioned. Such myths about Lang should finally be put to rest.[55]

Lang split from the Federal Labor Party in March 1931 because of its failure to endorse his Plan. All

New South Wales MLAs, a group of New South Wales Federal Members, and the great majority of unions and branches went with him. Theodore was expelled. The Federal authorities responded by expelling the Langites and setting up a rival Federal Branch in New South Wales.

Lang's stooges used physical violence to disrupt the New South Wales Federal Labor Party. LF Crisp has related how the diminutive General Secretary, Bill Colbourne, had the unnerving experience of crossing Sydney Harbour by ferry to address a meeting at Crows Nest sitting in the seat next to "five members of a 'basher gang' discussing their plans for assaulting him and his colleagues". Thus forewarned, Colbourne "arranged for the police to intervene the moment the gang moved into action. But the new Branch's speakers were not always so fortunate".[56]

On 25 November 1931, the Lang group in the Federal Parliament, alleging corruption by Theodore in the allocation of unemployment relief funds to his supporters, joined with the Opposition to bring down the Scullin Government. The leader of the Langites, Jack Beasley, acquired the enduring sobriquet of "Stabber Jack". The Scullin Government was decisively defeated at the December Federal election. In New South Wales, State Labor won 25 per cent of the primary vote and four seats compared to Federal Labor's 16 per cent and three seats. Theodore and future Labor Prime Minister Ben Chifley, an opponent of Lang, lost their seats. Chifley became President of the Federal Branch in 1934.[57]

Lang had ambitions to exploit the chaos in the Federal Party to seize the leadership. The Lang Plan was to be his battle standard. These hopes were largely illusory, and the bubble was pricked by Lang's failure to achieve complete electoral dominance in New South Wales at the 1931 Federal election.

The Lang Government increasingly struggled to meet its commitments. Desperate attempts to raise revenue were blocked by the Legislative Council. Lang's solution was debt repudiation. On 1 April 1931, he defaulted on interest repayments to British banks. The Scullin Government paid the interest, thus avoiding technical default.[58] The respite Lang gained was short-lived.

The government Savings Bank of New South Wales failed on 22 April after a run on its funds, with a calamitous effect on many small depositors. Schedvin has commented that it is "not entirely fair to infer that the closure of the Bank was due to Lang's policy. There is some truth in his allegation that the Nationalists were responsible by their claim during the October [1930] election campaign that the safety of deposits would in jeopardy under a Lang administration". However, the closure was precipitated by Lang's "failure to pay interest and principal due to the Bank during February and March, and by his default on overseas obligations".[59]

In June 1931, the Commonwealth and all State premiers adopted a deflationary plan to combat the economic crisis. The chief elements of what became known as the Premiers' Plan were cuts in government expenditure, increased taxation, and reduction of interest rates. Lang played a double game, agreeing to the Plan to obtain desperately needed finance from the Commonwealth but without a genuine commitment to its full implementation. He subsequently criticised the Premiers' Plan as inferior to the Lang Plan.[60]

Neville Cain has observed that, although the Premiers' Plan rejected Theodore's reflationary ideas, it was not as great a defeat for Theodore as is often assumed:

> Its retrenchment program was less severe than earlier proposals, and in an unprecedented Lang-like breach of contract, a statutory reduction of interest on internally held bonds was applied which—unlike contemporary wage cuts—would not be reversed as conditions improved. Moreover, during the protracted stand-off over budgetary policy, the Commonwealth Bank had been obliged to expand

credit significantly ... But his hopes of softening its impact with projects to relieve unemployment foundered upon banking intransigence.[61]

Lang was between a rock and a hard place: he could not implement the wage and expenditure cuts in the Premiers' Plan without alienating his base; his much-touted alternative Plan was unworkable. The inability to raise loan funds, the sharp decline in revenue and Lang's failure to reduce expenditure meant that the financial position of New South Wales became increasingly critical. The budget deficit for 1931/32 was a massive £14.2 million.[62] On 6 August 1931, 23,000 New South Wales public servants were not paid their fortnightly salary.

The effect on the community of the rapidly deteriorating financial position of New South Wales was disastrous and destabilising:

> The State's finances seemed to be on the verge of collapse. Child endowment cheques and other pensions were not honoured. Ominous announcements were made to the effect that all State services may soon have to cease. The salaries of State public service employees were one matter, but the implications of the non-payment of unemployment relief or police wages greatly concerned those who believed in maintaining 'law and order'. Minor panics had already occurred in some centres when food relief orders had been delayed.[63]

The ordinary people Lang claimed to be championing against British bondholders were suffering as a result of his actions.

In February 1932, Lang again defaulted on overseas interest repayments. This time, the default was actual as Joe Lyons' UAP Federal Government deliberately waited two weeks before meeting the obligation. Lang was once more foisting the New South Wales interest debt on to the Commonwealth to save him having to make unpopular cuts in expenditure. Lyons was determined to recoup the money owed by New South Wales and destroy Lang in the process. The *Financial Agreements Enforcement Act* was passed by the Federal Parliament and came into force on 12 March. It allowed the Commonwealth to recover directly from a State funds owed to it for interest repayments. Banks were required to pay to the Federal Government any funds belonging to New South Wales. All State revenue was also to be paid to the Commonwealth. In a pre-emptive move, Lang ordered that New South Wales assets be withdrawn from the banks and kept in the Treasury vaults. The public service was instructed to forward revenue to the Treasury rather than banking it. All government payments were to be via the Treasury, which became a *de facto* bank.[64] Lang unsuccessfully challenged the *Financial Agreements Enforcement Act* in the High Court. It was an obviously unsustainable situation. The financial health of New South Wales under Lang was entering the terminal phase.

This slide into financial chaos was accompanied by growing civil unrest. The inflammatory, populist rhetoric that Lang increasingly resorted to in an attempt to preserve the support of the Labor faithful exacerbated an already tense situation. Fears of class warfare and "Red revolution" became widespread among the middle and upper classes. Ordinary workers, the unemployed and the destitute became increasingly radicalised. Crisp has commented that after decades of full employment and prosperity it is difficult to "convey sufficiently vividly those 1931 days - the extreme tension, the grinding misery and desperation, the temper of the mass meetings and demonstrations of ill-fed, ill-clothed Lang adulators".[65]

WS Hamilton was a young journalist with the *Sun* newspaper. He went on to found the ABC News Service and became Assistant General Manager of the ABC. He has left this perceptive account of Sydney at the height of the Depression:

> It was a city unprepared for the misery with which it had so suddenly to cope. If your assignment was to do a feature on the hundreds of men sleeping under newspapers around Mrs Macquarie's Chair, it was something you had to do and you tried to feel nothing, or not too much. When the angry women threw clods of mud at the grim-faced policemen

> guarding endless evictions, you tried not to feel sorry for the policemen. It was a dirty job they had. You had a dirty job, too, to write about it, and you did it.[66]

Hamilton noted:

> The names you tossed around in the coffee shops were different now ... There were Jack Lang and boxing Billy McKell, and Bavin, the too gentle Opposition Leader, and Eric Campbell of the New Guard, Jock Garden, and Donald (later Senator) Grant, he who led the march of the workless on Parliament House only to fall foul of one of the best-planned coups of 'Big Bill' MacKay, that up-and-coming police officer everybody was whispering about ... Sydney had become a city of extremes and extremists, and it was ugly, even vicious, even if you were trained to feel nothing, but just to go about your business of reporting it, to keep out of the emotional whirlpools. But one thing you were sure about, whether you watched him from the press gallery, or tried to get a word with him, as he strode tempestuously through the corridors of the House, or just listened to the people, you knew that Jack Lang was the big name, dwarfing all the others as of right.[67]

This climate of upheaval and uncertainty produced a profound disillusionment on the conservative side of politics with the party and parliamentary systems. The All for Australia League, formed in February

1931, aimed to create national unity of purpose, to "set aside conflicting sectional interests" and to "exert constitutional pressure" on governments for balanced budgets and economy in public expenditure. By the end of June its membership was estimated to be 130,000. The All for Australia League's resentment of the influence of political parties made it, at first, hostile to the Nationalist Party. However, the fact that the League soon began to lose direction and momentum and the need to defeat Lang led to the League and the Nationalists merging as the United Australia Party in October 1931. In the process, the more radical policies of the All for Australia League disappeared. In April 1932, Bertram Stevens, a former senior bureaucrat in the Treasury who had been forced out by Lang, became Leader of the new Party.[68]

In country New South Wales, dissatisfaction with the existing political system expressed itself in the form of vigorous New State movements in the Riverina, the west and the north. The Riverina Movement was the most militant and radical, favouring the replacement of the State Parliament by self-governing provinces. In August 1931, the New State movements merged with the Country Party which renamed itself the United Country Party. There was much talk of unilateral secession at the height of the crises surrounding Lang.[69]

The most powerful exponent of the view that

the parliamentary system had failed and should be discarded was Eric Campbell's New Guard. A fascist-leaning, paramilitary organisation, it had a membership in 1931 of 36,000 in Sydney and 3,000 in the country. Its effective military strength has been estimated at just under 11,000. Andrew Moore in his definitive account of the Depression-era paramilitary groups says that on balance it "seems fair to conclude that the New Guard was about to fulfil its fascist potential but if Eric Campbell came perilously close to staging a fascist putsch in New South Wales the various splinter groups within the New Guard, especially the Fascist Legion, came even closer". There was regular street violence as New Guardsmen disrupted Communist meetings. However, Moore adds that by early 1932 "behind the bragging and bravado all the New Guard's weaknesses had become more pronounced. The movement's growing desire to mount a fascist putsch did not mean that this would succeed".[70]

The New Guard's moment of glory came on 19 March 1932. It was the day of the opening of the Sydney Harbour Bridge, a major architectural and engineering achievement. Lang decided to snub Governor Sir Philip Game by cutting the ribbon himself. The New Guard was outraged and one prominent member, Frank De Groot, decided to do something about it. WS Hamilton covered the event and left a vivid record:

I arrived at the well-guarded dais just before the first of the main dignitaries did. The dais began to fill and then the Premier himself took his place. It was quite a scene, but it wasn't my job to write it. It didn't look as if I was going to write anything, but a tiny worry was niggling my mind. Standing at the left of the dais, I finally watched the Governor-General, Sir Isaac Isaacs, drive up in his open coach, fore and aft the escort party of New South Wales Lancers, pennants fluttering, all polish and glitter. A brave show, but I had seen them before. Turning to go my eye lit on the officer at the rear of the escort party. He stood out, in an almost shabby field uniform, completely different from that of the Lancers, his horse rough-coated and uncurried. Trust the Army to foul it up, I thought. I couldn't claim that my suspicions were actually aroused, but my interest was. I had nothing else to write, I thought, so I might do a little par about the officer in the odd uniform. If I were quick I could possibly get a word with him. So, as the Lancers began to move off, I dodged around behind the dais and walked up the road towards the ribbon, leaving the speeches well behind. Nobody tried to stop me at first. I could see my quarry motionless, apparently in no hurry to get away. I was glancing around, left and right, when suddenly he dug his heels into his horse. I can still see that galvanic action. I started to run. Something was up. Out of the corner of my eye I glimpsed a policeman, spearing out from my right, arm outstretched, to cut me off. I swerved around him. Ahead of me, the horse was rearing wildly, two men (the police inspectors) reaching for its head. The officer's sword was raised high in the air. Down it came, down came the horse's plunging hooves, and down came de Groot, heavily to the ground, as MacKay pulled him from the saddle.[71]

More formidable and secretive was the Old Guard: the New Guard was a minnow thrashing on the surface, the Old Guard a submerged whale. Established by prominent figures in business, the professions and the pastoral industry, its aim was to protect the established order in case of civil unrest or insurrection, either from the New Guard or the Communist Party. Unlike the New Guard, the Old Guard's main strength was in the country, where it had an estimated 25,000 members across all regions compared to 5,000 in Sydney. By the end of 1931 it was:

> a colossus, possessing many times the combined manpower of the New South Wales police and the Commonwealth armed forces. It was efficiently and intricately organised, well-funded and armed, as well as being highly regarded in official circles…The primary objective was defensive, but throughout 1931 the organisation had become increasingly militant and prepared to take the offensive.[72]

If conflict occurred between New South Wales and the Commonwealth, it seems that the Lyons Government was prepared to swear in members of the Old Guard as Commonwealth Peace Officers to act as its auxiliaries.[73]

By May 1932, the situation had reached flashpoint. Large parts of rural New South Wales were threatening to secede unilaterally. The defence forces were mobilising for a possible confrontation with Lang. The Old Guard was committed to throwing its formidable resources behind the Commonwealth. The New Guard was plotting to seize Parliament House and forcibly overthrow the Lang Government. The New South Wales Police Force was ready to act as a military body to resist any attempted coup against Lang. "Big Bill" MacKay warned that the Police would use howitzers and grenades to repel any assault on Parliament House. To assist the Police, a plan had been developed to enroll thousands of public servants as special constables. A number of paramilitary Labor groups had been formed to defend the Lang Government. Although not as well organised and resourced as the right-wing paramilitaries, members of these organisations and militant unionists would have reacted violently to any attempt to overthrow Lang.[74]

Andrew Moore's assessment is that "civil strife really was quite close. Emotions ran very high. Tempers on all sides of the political spectrum were extremely frayed". There was a strong probability that "any violence would have snowballed in an alarming fashion".[75]

Dismissal

Governor Game strove mightily to be fair to Lang, to the point where he was snubbed in Sydney society. Articles in the press thunderously denounced him for not terminating Lang's Premiership.

Lang soon revived his attempt to abolish the Legislative Council and this time he had an electoral mandate. In December 1930, he demanded 80 appointments to the Upper House, almost doubling its size. Game refused, arguing that it was unjustified as the Council had not significantly impeded the Government's legislation. Lang repeatedly harassed the Governor for further appointments, but Game was unyielding.[76]

Lang sought to bypass Game by advising the King to instruct the Governor to act on the advice of his local ministers. The British Government supported Game. The Secretary of State for the Colonies advised that the New South Wales Government had:

> no right to advise the King directly and that when the King gave directions to a State Governor, he did so on the advice of British ministers. The Secretary of State acknowledged that the Governor had discretion in the exercise of his constitutional powers and stated that he was not prepared to advise the King to issue instructions to the Governor about how this discretion should be exercised.[77]

In November 1931, Lang moderated his request to 25 MLCs. This time, Game acquiesced:

> He accepted that the Legislative Council, perhaps emboldened by his previous refusals to swamp it, had been behaving unreasonably. He also recognised that Lang remained popular and had continued to win by-elections. Most importantly, however, Game saw these appointments as a tactical step to ward off future pressure for an even greater level of swamping of the Legislative Council. He thought that the appointment of 25 Members would ensure that most of Lang's legislation would be passed, except for the most extreme measures.[78]

The new appointees included the first female MLCs, Catherine Green and Ellen Webster. These appointments did not give Lang a reliable majority. He now had 42 MLCs and the Opposition 51. The balance of power was held by 16 MLCs loyal to Federal Labor and most were not well-disposed to Lang. Federal Labor was stronger among the MLCs as they had been appointed for life and thus were impervious to Lang's revenge.

There was now a further obstacle to abolition of the Council. The Bavin Government had inserted Section 7A in the Constitution providing that any measure abolishing the Council or changing its constitution and powers had to be approved by a referendum. The provision was entrenched so that it could only be removed by a referendum. Lang claimed Section 7A was invalid and in December 1930 passed legislation repealing it and abolishing the Council. The bills were struck down by the Supreme Court, supported on appeal by the High Court and the Privy Council.[79]

The political climate became even more feverish on 11 May 1932 when Lang suddenly introduced the Mortgages Taxation Bill. It imposed a tax of 10 per cent on the amount of a mortgage which had to be paid within 14 days. If the tax was not paid, the mortgage reverted to the Crown. The impact on "businesses and lenders such as banks had the potential to cause economic chaos. This was seen by many as the final catalyst for revolution".[80] As well as the wealthy, the legislation would have had a detrimental impact on many mortgage holders of moderate means.[81] Opposition Leader Stevens claimed the legislation was a payback for the *Financial Agreements Enforcement Act* and denounced it in incendiary terms:

> The Government's credit is gone. It cannot borrow money in the way that other governments can. Its public instrumentalities cannot borrow, because the Government's guarantee will not be accepted. The Government now says to the world, in a spirit of retaliation which suggests that it is prepared not only to defy constituted authority, but even to smash the entire fabric of our financial institutions,

> 'If we cannot get this money by means that are recognised as sound, according to the canons of British finance, we will adopt this foreign method, this revolutionary method, this destructive method of imposing a capital levy'.[82]

If implemented, it was estimated that the tax would have raised about £14 million. The Commonwealth Government immediately passed legislation to nullify the measure. The Mortgages Taxation Bill was never assented to and became irrelevant as Lang was dismissed from office on the day it was passed by the Legislative Council.

Game became increasingly concerned as the situation threatened to spin out of control. He was under enormous pressure to act. The Governor was, however, very aware of the need to behave constitutionally and impartially. The crisis point was reached on 13 May 1932.

In response to Lang's attempt to circumvent the *Financial Agreements Enforcement Act*, the Commonwealth on 6 May issued an instruction to New South Wales public servants directing them to pay all receipts into the Commonwealth Bank. On 10 May, Lang issued a circular confirming his earlier direction that State revenue was not to be paid into banks. Game concluded that this defiance of the Commonwealth was illegal. On 13 May, he asked Lang to prove his instructions to the public service were legal or withdraw them. Lang did not offer Crown legal advice on their validity or deny their illegality. He refused to withdraw the circulars. Later that day, Game told Lang that if he was not prepared to abide by the law he should resign. The Premier refused to do so and Game then used his reserve powers to dismiss him. He commissioned Stevens as caretaker Premier, who called an election for 11 June 1932.[83]

It has been argued that Game's action was improper as the alleged illegality of Lang's actions should have been resolved by the courts. Anne Twomey has provided a balanced assessment of the situation:

> It appears to be generally accepted that the Governor should not make himself or herself the judge of illegality so that, if a matter is justiciable, it should be dealt with by the courts. While this is certainly the correct principle, it must also be acknowledged that the circumstances giving rise to the potential exercise of this power [of dismissal] will always involve a crisis and most likely the serious potential for civil unrest, as was the case in 1932. In such cases, although the court system can work quickly to deal with important issues, the Governor may still be placed in a position where it is not possible to obtain a judicial verdict before action is needed. As with all conventions there must be some flexibility to deal with unusual circumstances.[84]

Nairn's view is that Game:

> could not allow New South Wales to cease to function as a stable society, with a 'solution' being effected by blood in the streets of Sydney and by dissolution in the country ... Inexorably, Lang had reached the limit of his ineptitude. His defiance of lawful constraints that was embodied in the circulars of 12 April and 10 May ... was basically a reflex of his demoralisation. It enabled Game to use the practical power he knew he possessed and which Lang did not dispute. The Governor did not dismiss the Premier because he was breaking the law, though that probability was an essential ingredient in the event as it evolved. Game dismissed Lang because he could no longer administer New South Wales.[85]

Lang accepted his dismissal and departed office peacefully.

Game believed that Lang had engineered his dismissal for political reasons. John Ward has supported this interpretation:

> For a Labor leader who had chosen the left, but principally wanted power and absolute control of policy, Lang was finding his position uncomfortable in 1932. Committed earlier by his own love of power to extreme policies needed to keep the left at his disposal, he had alienated too many of the moderate and right sections of the Party while not gratifying

the left. Dismissal from office on a constitutional ground relieved him from having to clear up the mess but leaving his reputation as a strong driving left wing (but anti-Communist) leader intact.[86]

It is possible that Lang was deluded enough to see his dismissal as a springboard for decisive re-election and a triumphant vindication that would have allowed him to dispose of his enemies, from the Governor on down, once and for all – a frightening prospect.

The 1932 election was one of the most hotly contested in New South Wales' history. Lang's dismissal galvanised his hard-core supporters and the party faithful. A mass meeting at Moore Park in Sydney's eastern suburbs on 5 June was attended by 200,000 according to the police. The Lang Party claimed the crowd numbered 750,000. According to the *Sydney Morning Herald*:

> The crowd was probably the largest which has ever gathered at a political rally in New South Wales. It began to assemble in the morning, hours before the meeting was timed to open. At 2 o'clock there was a dense mass of men, women and children about the lorry from which Mr Lang was to speak. Mrs Lang and her daughter mounted the lorry half an hour before the rest of the party arrived at the head of the procession, and Mrs Lang was kept busy autographing hundreds of mirrors detached from women's handbags, and other souvenirs, as was Mr

Lang after he had arrived.[87]

Lang whipped up the audience with his usual histrionics:

> This magnificent demonstration is a fitting answer to those who are attempting to set up a despotic rule in this State. By the illegal and arbitrary use of the Governor's position, they have driven the people's representatives out of Parliament. (Hoots.) They have banned the people's cause from the pages of the metropolitan newspapers, and they have driven the people's movement out of the people's Domain. (Renewed hoots.) Should they succeed in carrying their plans any further, they will drive your unmarried daughters into unemployed shelters; they will conscript your unmarried sons into unemployed camps; they will smash down your standards of living, and break up your family circle. They will not succeed. (Cries of 'No, no'.) They will not succeed because I believe that on Saturday next my fellow Australians, with an almost unanimous effort, will send back into our Parliament the people's party (Cheers), and with a unanimous voice will demand that no Governor shall ever again usurp the rights of the people; that a press, which is not free and just, has no right to exist (Hear, hear); that the Australian standard of living must be preserved at all costs; and that the conscription of the young men and women of this country shall never be permitted in any war, whether that war be waged by a hostile race or the

bankers within our shores.[88]

Stevens described Lang's Moore Park speech as the desperate last throw:

> of a political desperado and outlaw caught red-handed at the scene of his political crimes. The Socialist Leader's speech was one blind appeal to mob passion and class hate. Mr Lang trotted out the old bogeys which had served him so well in the past. He supported them by untruths. To the great body of the people I say there is not one atom of truth or fact in the prophecies of Mr Lang ... If the Lang Government were given a new lease of life, civil servants, pensioners, mothers and widows would again face a payless dawn. Mr Lang says that we would attempt to fasten the slave conditions of Central Europe upon our people. Mr Lang and his colleagues who adopted the Socialisation Policy have declared for revolution and the overthrow of government by the people. They alone would introduce European conditions. Socialisation has reduced the Russian farmer to slavery, and the Russian worker to a national dole ticket system.[89]

Both campaigns were based on fear and hope. Stevens claimed that Lang would further impoverish the State and lead it towards socialism and Communism. A Coalition Government would restore sound finance and prosperity, and safeguard traditional rights and freedoms. Lang branded Stevens a ruthless exploiter of the workers and agent of the financiers. Only Lang could be trusted to protect wages and social services.

The election result was a decisive repudiation of Lang. Labor won 24 seats compared to 55 in 1930. The primary vote dropped from 56 per cent to 40 per cent. Federal Labor polled 4 per cent and won no seats. The Stevens-Bruxner Coalition had 64 seats with 49 per cent of the vote (there were also two UAP/UCP MLAs). According to Hagan and Turner's regional analysis, Labor support collapsed in the western country area, from 14 seats to none, and in suburban Sydney, from 19 to four.[90]

Ben Chifley summed up Lang's second Premiership perceptively:

> Mr Lang used the State Labor Party not as a vehicle to further the interests of the people, but as an incense-burner to further his own vanity. Instead of facing the situation, using common sense and, if necessary, even suffering some unpopularity, Mr Lang spent his time tickling the ears of the unfortunate sections of the people who were themselves so distracted by their position they were prepared to chase any economic rainbows – and Mr Lang provided a number of those rainbows.[91]

Downfall

Lang made up little ground at the May 1935 New South Wales election, gaining only five seats. In March 1938, Labor actually went backwards, winning one less seat, 28 compared to 29 in 1935 (Heffron Labor had two seats). The Party was so debilitated that it contested only 51 of the 90 electorates. Lang's electoral appeal was evaporating and was largely confined to zealots and inner city blue-collar workers. Between 1931-38, he performed poorly in three Federal elections, lost three State and Sydney Municipal Council elections, and unsuccessfully opposed the 1934 referendum to reform the Legislative Council.[92] Lang was increasingly seen by many Laborites as "the man of repeated defeats and of chronically divisive propensities".[93]

Lang's position was further undermined by slow but steady recovery from the depths of the Depression and the fact that, contrary to Lang's dire predictions, Stevens governed in a moderate way. John McCarthy has said:

> Stevens should be seen by those on the left of politics a shade less darkly. There were many of the right who had a much lower concern for those who, devoid of protection, became victims of the Depression. There were those in the Government and outside it who wished to see the labour movement destroyed. Stevens did not accept that proposition.[94]

In spite of his defeats, Lang had no intention of relinquishing his iron grip on New South Wales Labor. He had a victory in February 1936 when a unity conference called by the Federal Executive recognised the Lang Party as the New South Wales Branch. The Federal Branch under Chifley and Colbourne had fought Lang resolutely but was outnumbered and under-resourced. Political expediency was also against it. New Federal Leader John Curtin was keen to heal the electorally damaging schism in New South Wales. The downside for Lang was that he acknowledged the authority of the Federal Party. A condition of the deal was that Colbourne be kept on as an organiser. As good a hater as ever, Lang reneged and dismissed him.[95]

Lang steadily lost union support. As his power slipped away, he lashed out at allies "who had outlived their usefulness for him, or who seemed likely to rival him, or otherwise irritated him".[96] Willis and Garden fell out with Lang and were vilified and expelled.

In August 1936, the Trades and Labor Council organised a conference to press for reform of the party. Lang and his Inner Group were strongly attacked by many speakers. The Inner Group responded by calling a special conference which expelled 16 union officials and five State Members involved with the conference. They were subsequently reinstated by the Federal Executive.

In early 1938 the anti-Lang forces formed a rival Party and Executive, claiming to be the legitimate Labor Party. After a long legal struggle, the rebels wrested control of the *Labor Daily* from Lang in February 1938, a serious blow to his domination of the party. Lang started his own newspaper, *Century*. The new group was known as the Industrialist or Heffron Party, after Bob Heffron, MLA for Botany, who was its leader. Crisp has observed that, unlike the breakaway Lang Branch, the Heffron Party "was not challenging Federal authority, but rather joining with the ACTU and AWU in seeking Federal intervention once more to secure a basis for lasting unity in New South Wales – by implication by eliminating Lang".[97]

Heffron initially had support from only one other MLA, CC Lazzarini (Marrickville), but was later joined by the two Broken Hill members, MA Davidson (Cobar) and EM Horsington (Sturt). The parliamentary ranks, and the Heffron Party in general, were given a big boost at two by-elections in early 1939. Hurstville and Waverley, both marginal Sydney suburban electorates, were won from the UAP by Heffron candidates (Clive Evatt and Clarrie Martin respectively) in the face of strong Lang opposition. These victories were a major turning point as they clearly demonstrated that Lang's electoral appeal had evaporated. In June,

Frank Burke (Newtown) joined the Heffron group bringing its strength to seven MLAs compared to Lang's 25. Although Lang had virtually no union support, he would seem to have been stronger than the Industrialists in the branches.

The electorally damaging divisions in New South Wales forced the Federal Executive to intervene. The supporters of both parties came together at a conference controlled by Federal officials to determine who was to rule in New South Wales. The unity conference, which met on 26 August 1939, was a rout for the "Langsters". They were defeated on an early vote by 211 to 153.[98] It was a victory for those who wanted to restore Labor's heritage as a democratic organisation committed to moderate reform through the parliamentary process.

The conference disposed of Lang by returning the right to elect the leader to the parliamentarians, the majority of whom despised him. Although Heffron had spearheaded the fight against Lang, the moderate, experienced Bill McKell had the numbers. In the Caucus ballot on 5 September 1939, McKell had 13 votes, Lang 12 and Heffron seven. All of Heffron's preferences flowed to McKell who was elected leader 20 to 13.

There were three main factions within the "reunited" ALP: a group of anti-Lang and anti-

Communist union officials who supported McKell, Lang's supporters, and covert Communists.

Communists were heavily involved in the struggle to depose Lang and, as a result, were able to infiltrate the Labor Party, notably New South Wales Vice President Jack Hughes and Secretary Bill Evans. Matters came to a head at the March 1940 annual conference when a motion was passed opposing any aggressive act against the Soviet Union. The so-called "Hands off Russia" resolution allowed Lang to take centre stage and call for immediate Federal intervention to rid the Party of Communist influence. The Lang faction had actually voted for the resolution to flush the Communists into the open.

When the Federal Executive refused to accede to Lang's demands, he used this as an excuse to defect and form the Australian Labor Party (Non-Communist) in April 1940. It had little union backing but did have the support of five MHRs, two Senators, nine MLAs and six MLCs. Lang had always been anti-Communist and seized on the "Red menace" to differentiate his Party and give it an issue to campaign on.

Although the Federal Executive was determined not to dance to Lang's tune, it realised that the Communist cabal had to be dealt with and in August 1940 once again reconstructed the New South Wales Branch. The group of anti-Lang and anti-Communist union officials who took over remained in control of the Labor Party until 1952. The formation of a new breakaway group, the State or Hughes-Evans Labor Party, followed. It had no parliamentary supporters and, as the September 1940 Federal elections demonstrated, little electoral popularity. In the face of significant gains by the ALP (five seats in New South Wales), it never appeared likely to win a seat. After its banning in June 1940, the Communist Party made much use of the State Labor Party for its public campaigns. Individual Communists stood as State Labor candidates in the 1941 New South Wales election, for example, Hughes himself in Bankstown, Sam Lewis in Randwick and Rupert Lockwood in Concord. The Party polled an insignificant 6 per cent. The Hughes-Evans Party merged with the Communist Party in 1943.

The 1940 Federal election had also been a disappointment to Lang's Non-Communist Labor Party. The Langites won 13 per cent of the vote compared to the ALP's 35 per cent. Confronted with the prospect of withering into oblivion, Lang decided to unite with Official Labor. A committee of Non-Communist Labor Party members negotiated the amalgamation of branches with the Official Party Executive. All Non-Communist MLAs were endorsed as ALP candidates. Lang was the last to sign a loyalty pledge on 24 February 1941.

A section of the former Non-Communist Labor Party, however, was unhappy with the way unity was being achieved. A meeting at Newtown Town Hall heard complaints that former Non-Communist branches were being swamped by Official Party members in the amalgamation process and that representation at the annual conference was inadequate. Lang was bitterly attacked for selling-out his supporters. This led to the formation in April of yet another breakaway Labor Party, confusingly called the Australian Labor Party. Delegates from 20 former Non-Communist branches attended the meeting that formed the new party. It contested four seats in the 1941 election, Balmain, Botany, Cook's River and Newtown, unsuccessfully in all cases.

McKell easily won the election held on 10 May 1941, with 54 of the 90 seats and 51 per cent of the primary vote. Lang was not content to remain an insignificant backbencher for long. An obsessive mischief-maker as always, he commenced a campaign of harassment and dissent against McKell in Caucus, parliament and through his newspaper *Century*. It is conceivable that Lang was so far out of touch with reality that he believed he could make a come-back.[99] The Executive responded by expelling him in February 1943. Lang's expulsion was confirmed by the June annual conference.

Lang re-formed his Non-Communist Labor Party.

At the 1944 New South Wales election he retained Auburn and his disciple Lillian Fowler won Newtown. The Non-Communist Labor vote was 9 per cent compared to the ALP's 46 per cent. The strong performance of the McKell Government had made Lang irrelevant.

In 1946, Lang decided to move to the Commonwealth Parliament and was elected MHR for Reid, which contained his State seat of Auburn. His son, John Christian, won Auburn at the ensuing by-election. At the 1950 State election, both JC Lang and Fowler were defeated. Lang Labor was never to have a presence in the New South Wales Legislative Assembly again.

In Canberra, Lang was a frequent, rancorous critic of Chifley. Lang had never forgiven Chifley for contesting his seat of Auburn as the Federal Labor candidate at the 1935 New South Wales election. Lang lost Reid in 1949 and failed in a bid for the Senate in 1951. It was the end of his parliamentary career.

Epilogue

Lang devoted the rest of his long life to defending and embellishing his record. Egotistical self-justification and the pursuit of grudges were much in evidence. He produced a series of memoirs, almost certainly not written by him,[100] notable for self-aggrandisement and inaccuracy. Lang continued to publish *Century*, regularly attacking almost everything the Federal and New South Wales governments (of whatever political persuasion) did. It was also a source of malicious gossip and scurrilous misinformation.

In person, Lang harangued any person or group prepared to listen about his achievements. Michael Maher (State MP for Drummoyne 1973-82 and Federal Member for Lowe 1982-87) invited Lang to speak at a function during his first campaign. Maher recalled: "He spoke for about an hour and a half about what he did and then he said 'Oh, by the way, there's a fellow here running for this seat. He looks a clean-cut type of candidate – vote for him' and sat down".[101]

In 1962, the 18-year-old Paul Keating became a disciple: "Twice a week for the next eight years, he helped the old warhorse with the proofs of his paper and soaked up Labor lore, tales of treason and loyalty larded with Lang's take-no -prisoners philosophy".[102] At the 1970 New South Wales annual conference, Keating pressed for Lang's readmission but was thwarted by Lang's old enemy Bill Colbourne. The next year Keating tried again, this time successfully. However, Colbourne had the motion amended so that instead of being triumphally readmitted by the conference, Lang had to join his local branch in the ordinary way, which he did.

Jack Lang died on 27 September 1975, just short of his 99th birthday. In retrospect, Lang's positive achievements, such as widows' pensions, child endowment and the moratorium legislation in the Depression, are outweighed by the negative. He devastated the Labor Party, created bitter social divisions, almost bankrupted the State, and brought New South Wales to the brink of civil war.

Endnotes

1. See David Clune, *Sir William McKell*, Connor Court, Redland Bay, 2021. Labor was in office from 1941-65, 1976-88 and 1995-2011.

2. This account of Lang's early life draws on Bede Nairn, *The 'Big Fella': Jack Lang and the Australian Labor Party 1891-1949*, Melbourne University Press, Carlton, 1986.

3. By Jock Garden in 1933. See Nairn, *The 'Big Fella': Jack Lang and the Australian Labor Party 1891-1949*, p. 269.

4. Peter Spearritt, "The Auburn plute" in Heather Radi and Peter Spearritt eds, *Jack Lang*, Sydney, Hale and Iremonger and Labour History, Sydney, 1977, p. 6.

5. Bede Nairn, "Lang, John Thomas (Jack) (1876–1975)" *Australian Dictionary of Biography*, National Centre of Biography, Australian National University, http://adb.anu.edu.au/biography/lang-john-thomas-jack-7027/text12223, published first in hardcopy 1983, accessed online 26 December 2020.

6. Nairn, *The 'Big Fella': Jack Lang and the Australian Labor Party 1891-1949*, p. 38.

7. *New South Wales Parliamentary Debates*, 3 March 1914, pp. 18-20.

8. Peter Spearritt, "The Auburn plute" in Heather Radi and Peter Spearritt (eds), *Jack Lang*, p. 21.

9. *New South Wales Parliamentary Debates*, 29 August 1917, p. 824.

10. *Sydney Morning Herald*, 19 September 1919.

11. See Jim Hagan, "John Storey" and Duncan Waterson, "James Dooley" in David Clune and Ken Turner, (eds), *The Premiers of New South Wales, 1856-2005*, vol 2, Federation Press, Leichhardt, 2006.

12. *New South Wales Parliamentary Debates*, 30 August 1917, p. 896.

13. Nairn, *The 'Big Fella': Jack Lang and the Australian Labor Party 1891-1949*, p. 41.

14. Murray Perks, "The rise to leadership" in Radi and Spearritt (eds), *Jack Lang*, p. 29.

15 Waterson, "James Dooley" in Clune and Turner (eds), *The Premiers of New South Wales, 1856-2005*, p. 162.

16 Perks, "The rise to leadership" in Radi and Spearritt eds, *Jack Lang*, pp. 32-36.

17 Ibid., p. 37.

18 Nairn, *The 'Big Fella': Jack Lang and the Australian Labor Party 1891-1949*, pp. 61-6.

19 Ibid., pp. 71-2.

20 See David Clune, "Sir George Warburton Fuller" in Clune and Turner (eds), *The Premiers of New South Wales*.

21 *New South Wales Parliamentary Debates*, 12 August 1925, pp. 66-71.

22 *New South Wales Parliamentary Debates*, 3 September 1925, p. 543.

23 *New South Wales Parliamentary Debates*, 26 November 1925, pp. 2588-2592.

24 *Sydney Morning Herald*, 6 March 1926.

25 Nairn, *The 'Big Fella': Jack Lang and the Australian Labor Party 1891-1949*, p. 287.

26 David Clune and Gareth Griffith, *Decision and Deliberation: the Parliament of New South Wales, 1856-2003*, Federation Press, Leichhardt, 2006, p. 246.

27 For an analysis of the legislative record see Helen Nelson, "Legislative record, 1925-27. How radical?" and Fran Jelley "Child endowment" in Heather Radi and Peter Spearritt eds, *Jack Lang*.

28 Anne Twomey, "Sir Dudley Rawson Stratford De Chair" in David Clune and Ken Turner (eds), *The Governors of New South Wales, 1788-2010*, Federation Press, Leichhardt, 2009, pp. 463-7.

29 Anne Twomey, *The Veiled Sceptre: reserve powers of heads of state in Westminster systems*, Cambridge University Press, Melbourne, 2018, p. 724.

30 Nairn, *The 'Big Fella': Jack Lang and the Australian Labor Party 1891-1949*, pp. 127-8.

31 Ibid., pp. 126-7.

32 Ibid., pp. 136-47.

33	Anne Twomey, "Sir Dudley Rawson Stratford De Chair" in Clune and Turner (eds), *The Governors of New South Wales, 1788-2010*, pp. 467-9.
34	Nairn, *The 'Big Fella': Jack Lang and the Australian Labor Party 1891-1949*, pp. 147-52.
35	Ibid., p. 155.
36	Kevin Cosgrove, "1927" in Michael Hogan and David Clune eds, *The People's Choice: electoral politics in twentieth century New South Wales*, vol 1, Parliament of New South Wales and University of Sydney, 2001, p. 368.
37	Nairn, *The 'Big Fella': Jack Lang and the Australian Labor Party 1891-1949*, pp. 83-5, 190-91.
38	Ibid., pp. 193-6, 268-9.
39	See John Paul, "Thomas Rainsford Bavin" in Clune and Turner (eds), *The Premiers of New South Wales, 1856-2005*, vol 2.
40	Boris Schedvin, *Australia and the Great Depression*, Sydney University Press, Sydney, 1970, p. 188.
41	Reproduced in Clune and Turner (eds), *The Premiers of New South Wales, 1856-2005*, vol 2.
42	Boris Schedvin, *Australia and the Great Depression*, p. 47.
43	Ibid., p. 176.
44	*Official Year Book of New South Wales, 1932-33*, NSW Government Printer, Sydney.
45	Peter Love, "Frank Anstey and the monetary radicals" in RT Appleyard and Boris Schedvin, eds *Australian Financiers: biographical essays*, Macmillan, South Melbourne, 1988, p. 268.
46	Ibid., p. 268.
47	Boris Schedvin, *Australia and the Great Depression*, p180-8; Bede Nairn, *The 'Big Fella': Jack Lang and the Australian Labor Party 1891-1949*, p. 205.
48	Ibid., p. 226.
49	Neville Cain, "Theodore, Edward Granville (1884–1950)" *Australian Dictionary of Biography*, National Centre of Biography, Australian National University, http://adb.anu.edu.au/biography/theodore-edward-granville-8776/text15385, published first in hardcopy 1990, accessed online 2 January 2021.

50 Peter Love, "Frank Anstey and the monetary radicals" in Appleyard and Schedvin (eds), *Australian Financiers: Biographical Essays*, p. 268.

51 KH Kennedy, "EG Theodore" in Appleyard and Schedvin (eds), *Australian Financiers: Biographical Essays*, p. 298.

52 Boris Schedvin, *Australia and the Great Depression*, p. 230. The reference to "economic rainbows" is from Ben Chifley. See L. F. Crisp, *Ben Chifley*, Longmans, Melbourne, 1961, p. 66.

53 Bede Nairn, "A view of Jack Lang and his role in Labor history to 1939" in ALP (New South Wales), *Traditions for Reform in New South Wales*, Pluto, Sydney, 1987, p. 59. On the Lang Plan see also Alex Millmow, *The Power of Economic Ideas: the origins of Keynesian macroeconomic management in interwar Australia 1929–39*, ANU Press, Canberra, 2010, p. 86.

54 David Clark, "Was Lang right?" in Radi and Spearritt (eds), *Jack Lang*, p. 139.

55 Ibid., p. 158.

56 L. F. Crisp, *Ben Chifley*, p. 74.

57 Ibid., pp. 82-4.

58 Under the Financial Agreement of 1927 between the Commonwealth and States, the Commonwealth took responsibility for State debts. The Loan Council (established as a voluntary body in 1923) was given the sole responsibility to raise future loans for the Commonwealth and States.

59 Boris Schedvin, Australia and the Great Depression, p. 235.

60 Ibid., pp. 248-52.

61 Neville Cain, "Theodore, Edward Granville (1884–1950)" *Australian Dictionary of Biography*, National Centre of Biography, Australian National University, http://adb.anu.edu.au/biography/theodore-edward-granville-8776/text15385, published first in hardcopy 1990, accessed online 2 January 2021.

62 Boris Schedvin, *Australia and the Great Depression*, p. 273.

63 Andrew Moore, *The Secret Army and the Premier*, UNSW Press, Sydney, 1989, pp. 168-9.

64 Boris Schedvin, *Australia and the Great Depression*, pp. 351-3.

65 L.F. Crisp, *Ben Chifley*, p. 74.

66 *Sydney Morning Herald*, 4 March 1972.

67 *Sydney Morning Herald*, 4 March 1972.

68 See Peter Loveday, "Anti-political political thought" and Trevor Matthews, "The All for Australia League" in *Labour History*, No. 17, 1970.

69 Don Aitkin, *The Colonel: a political biography of Sir Michael Bruxner*, ANU Press, Canberra, 1969, pp. 136-9.

70 Moore, *The Secret Army and the Premier*, pp. 147-8, 183-4.

71 *Sydney Morning Herald*, 4 March 1972. See also Andrew Moore, *Francis De Groot: Irish fascist, Australian legend*, Federation Press, Leichhardt, 2005.

72 Moore, *The Secret Army and the Premier*, pp. 82-103, 135-6.

73 Ibid., pp. 189-206.

74 This paragraph is based on Andrew Moore, *The Secret Army and the Premier*.

75 Ibid., p. 206.

76 Anne Twomey, "Sir Philip Woolcott Game" in Clune and Turner (eds), *The Governors of New South Wales, 1788-2010*, pp. 477-81.

77 Anne Twomey, "Sir Philip Woolcott Game" in Clune and Turner (eds), *The Governors of New South Wales, 1788-2010*, p. 481.

78 Ibid., pp. 482-3.

79 Anne Twomey, *The Constitution of New South Wales*, Federation Press, Leichhardt, 2004, pp. 368-9.

80 Anne Twomey, "Sir Philip Woolcott Game" in Clune and Turner (eds), *The Governors of New South Wales, 1788-2010*, p. 487.

81 Nairn, *The 'Big Fella': Jack Lang and the Australian Labor Party 1891-1949*, pp. 259-60.

82 *New South Wales Parliamentary Debates*, 11 May 1932, p. 9276.

83 Anne Twomey, *The Veiled Sceptre: reserve powers of heads of state in Westminster systems*, pp. 312-8; Anne Twomey, "Sir Philip Woolcott Game" in Clune and Turner (eds), *The Governors of New South Wales, 1788-2010*, pp. 486-9.

84 Anne Twomey, *The Constitution of New South Wales*, p646. See also Anne Twomey, "The dismissal of the Lang Government" in George Winterton (ed), *State Constitutional Landmarks*, Federation Press, Leichhardt, 2006.

85 Nairn, *The 'Big Fella': Jack Lang and the Australian Labor Party 1891-1949*, pp. 260-1.

86 John Manning Ward, "The dismissal" in Radi and Spearritt (eds), *Jack Lang*, p. 177.

87 *Sydney Morning Herald*, 6 June 1932.

88 Ibid.

89 *Sun*, 6 June 1932.

90 Jim Hagan and Ken Turner, *A History of the Labor Party in New South Wales, 1891-1991*, Longman Cheshire, South Melbourne, 1991, pp. 261-2.

91 Quoted in L. F. Crisp, *Ben Chifley*, p. 66.

92 Bede Nairn, "Lang, John Thomas (Jack) (1876–1975)" *Australian Dictionary of Biography*, http://adb.anu.edu.au/biography/lang-john-thomas-jack-7027/text12223, published first in hardcopy 1983, accessed online 26 December 2020.

93 L. F. Crisp, *Ben Chifley*, p. 105.

94 John McCarthy, "Bertram Sydney Barnsdale Stevens" in Clune and Turner (eds), *The Premiers of New South Wales, 1856-2005*, vol 2, p. 233.

95 L. F. Crisp, *Ben Chifley*, pp. 99-103; David Clune, "Colbourne, William Regis (Bill) (1895–1979)", *Australian Dictionary of Biography*, https://adb.anu.edu.au/biography/colbourne-william-regis-bill-12848/text23195, published first in hardcopy 2005, accessed online 27 March 2021.

96 Nairn, *The 'Big Fella': Jack Lang and the Australian Labor Party 1891-1949*, p. 269.

97 L. F. Crisp, *Ben Chifley*, p. 105.

98 Nairn, *The 'Big Fella': Jack Lang and the Australian Labor Party 1891-1949*, pp. 300-2.

99 In the 1941 campaign, Lang was reported as saying he hoped to lead Labor again. He subsequently denied making the statement. *Sydney Morning Herald*, 9 May 1941.

100 The author was probably AC Paddison. Bede Nairn, "Lang, John Thomas (Jack) (1876–1975)" *Australian Dictionary of Biography*, http://adb.anu.edu.au/biography/lang-john-thomas-jack-7027/text12223, published first in hardcopy 1983, accessed online 26 December 2020.

101 David Clune, "Michael Maher: a good local Member" in Ken Turner and Michael Hogan (eds), *The Worldly Art of Politics*, Federation Press, Leichhardt, 2006, p. 47.

102 Shane Maloney and Chris Grosz, "Paul Keating and Jack Lang" in *The Monthly*, April 2009.

Select Bibliography

Frank Cain, *Jack Lang: and the Great Depression*, Australian Scholarly Publishing, Melbourne, 2005.

David Clune and Gareth Griffith, *Decision and Deliberation: the Parliament of NSW, 1856-2003*, Federation Press, Leichhardt, 2006.

David Clune and Ken Turner eds, *The Governors of NSW, 1788-2010*, Federation Press, Leichhardt, 2009.

David Clune and Ken Turner eds, *The Premiers of NSW, 1856-2005*, vol 2, Federation Press, Leichhardt, 2006.

Robert Cooksey, *Lang and Socialism: a study in the Great Depression*, Australian National University Press, 1971.

Leslie Finlay Crisp, *Ben Chifley*, Longman, Victoria, 1961.

Miriam Dixson, *Greater Than Lenin? Lang and Labour 1916-1932*, Melbourne Politics Monograph, number 4, Melbourne University, Political Science Department, 1976.

Bethia Foott, *Dismissal of a Premier: the Philip Game papers*, Morgan, Sydney, 1968.

Jim Hagan and Ken Turner, *A History of the Labor Party in New South Wales, 1891-1991*, Longman Cheshire, South Melbourne, 1991.

Michael Hogan and David Clune eds, *The People's Choice: electoral politics in twentieth century NSW*, vols 1 and 2, Parliament of NSW and University of Sydney, 2001.

Andrew Moore, *Francis De Groot: Irish fascist, Australian legend*, Federation Press, Leichhardt, 2005.

Andrew Moore, *The Secret Army and the Premier*, University of NSW Press, 1989.

Bede Nairn, *The 'Big Fella'. Jack Lang and the Australian Labor Party 1891-1949*, Melbourne University Press, 1986.

Heather Radi and Peter Spearritt eds, *Jack Lang*, Sydney, Hale and Iremonger and Labour History, Neutral Bay, 1977.

Don Rawson, "The Organisation of the Australian Labor Party 1916-1941", unpublished PhD thesis, University of Melbourne, 1954.

John Robertson, *JH Scullin: a political biography*, University of Western Australia Press, Nedlands, WA, 1974.

Boris Schedvin, *Australia and the Great Depression*, Sydney University Press, 1971.

Anne Twomey, *The Constitution of NSW*, Federation Press, Leichhardt, 2004.

Anne Twomey, "The Dismissal of the Lang Government" in George Winterton ed, *State Constitutional Landmarks*, Federation Press, Leichhardt, 2006.

All election results are from Colin Hughes and Bruce Graham, *A Handbook of Australian Government and Politics 1890-1964*, ANU Press, Canberra, 1968.

www.ingramcontent.com/pod-product-compliance
Lightning Source LLC
Chambersburg PA
CBHW071500160426
43195CB00013B/2168